Radical Forgiveness
Through the Eyes of Jesus

Floyd Bland

© 2018 by Floyd W. Bland. All rights reserved. No portion of this book may be reproduced in any form without permission from the publisher, except as permitted by U.S. copyright law. For permissions, contact: info@notwm.org

The views expressed in this book are those of the author and are intended for Christian discipleship purposes only. Every effort has been made to ensure that the content provided is helpful for our readers at press time. However, this book is not intended to be an exhaustive treatment of the subject matter. No liability is assumed for losses or damages due to the information provided. The author and publisher advise readers to take full responsibility for their safety and wellbeing.

The author is not engaged in rendering legal or clinical advice in any manner. If clinical or legal advice is required, the services of a competent professional should be sought.

Some content has been recreated from events, locales, and conversations from the author's memory. Unless otherwise specified, all names, places, identifying characteristics, and details have been significantly altered to maintain anonymity. Any resemblance to actual persons, living or dead, businesses, events, or locales is purely coincidental.

Scriptures marked KJV are taken from the King James Version (KJV): King James Version, public domain.

Scripture quotations marked (NLT) are taken from the Holy Bible, New Living Translation, copyright ©1996, 2004, 2015 by Tyndale House Foundation. Used by permission of Tyndale House Publishers, Inc., Carol Stream, Illinois 60188. All rights reserved.

Scripture quotations marked (NIV) are taken from the Holy Bible, New International Version®, NIV®. Copyright © 1973, 1978, 1984, 2011 by Biblica, Inc.™ Used by permission of Zondervan. All rights reserved worldwide. www.zondervan.com. The "NIV" and "New International Version" are trademarks registered in the United States Patent and Trademark Office by Biblica, Inc.™

The images used for chapter headings are officially licensed from ©Graphics Factory.com.

ISBN-13: 978-0-9909823-4-0

Because He Lives!

Contents

With Gratitude: viii

Introduction: Discovering God's Forgiveness   1

Chapter 1: Four Important Lessons   13
    Who Am I? Listen To Him! Who Is The Greatest? Seventy Times Seven

Chapter 2: The Forgiving King   28
    A Massive Debt Is Forgiven, Why We Need Forgiveness, Our Debt Is Canceled Forever

Chapter 3: The Servant Is Restored   39
    A New Spiritual Being, God Declares Us Righteous, We Have God's Spirit inside Us, We Have Eternal Fellowship with God, Our Access Is Restored

Chapter 4: The Unforgiving Servant   51
    We Are Equal Debtors, We Help and Support Each Other, We Have Cordial, Meaningful Relationships, We Love One Another, We Forgive One Another

Chapter 5: On To Radical Forgiveness   66
    Our Freedom in Christ, We Are Crucified With Christ, On To Radical Forgiveness

About The Author   76

With Gratitude

I thank God for His grace and mercy. He sent His Son to die for my sins and raised Him for my justification. Then He sent His Spirit to secure my eternal future that He has prepared for all those who love His glorious appearing (2 Timothy 4:8).

For my Christian home with parents whose love, faith, and piety yet inspire me to live for Christ, along with my loving, affirming, and supportive wife and family. I thank God for all of you!

To my extended family, those who encouraged me to continue writing, and to those who helped with the book's cover and editing, I am grateful to God for you as well.

Introduction
Discovering God's Forgiveness

Whenever I reflect on my life's journey, I marvel at how the Lord has been gracious and merciful to me over the years. I can attribute my spiritual journey to the combined efforts of three very extraordinary people who led me to the Lord Jesus Christ and helped understand His Kingdom living.

Mom, Dad, and Grandma were the perfect instruments the Lord used to raise me in His "nurture and admonition." (Ephesians 6:4 KJV) First, they loved me enough to introduce me to the Lord early in life. Then they took the time to explain fundamental biblical truths in a way that allowed me to understand and grow from them.

What I appreciated the most was they loved the Lord enough to model His exceptional Christian character in front of me consistently. They were not perfect; none of us are. But they were amazingly consistent.

Born before the Great Depression, Mom was the "fighter." I admired her courage and fortitude as she often spoke of how hard she struggled to obtain the things of value to her and the family.

Before I met my wife, Mom was my best friend and confidant who shared many inspirational stories I remember and treasure today.

Stories of her childhood in the South, helping Grandma and Grandpa provide for their poor southern family, moving up North, her experiences during the war years (WWII), graduating from high school, meeting and marrying Dad, and moving out West still resonate within me.

One common thread: "The Lord is faithful, and He'll provide for His children" (see: Genesis 22:14), would always emerge from her inspiring stories.

Another pre-Depression baby was Dad. He was the "leader" who showed me "If God is for us, then who can be against us?" as Romans 8:31 teaches.

I cannot remember if he ever told me if he graduated from high school. He was like the many other African-American southern youth who started working as a child and then served in the Armed Forces during the War (WWII).

I watched him lead us to church every Sunday and in our regular family devotions. His was the comforting voice I heard when he arrived home at the end of his workday. He was the one who prayed the blessing over the meal at the breakfast and dinner tables.

Although Mom and Grandma were quite capable, his was the switch (or belt) I felt most often when I needed corrective discipline. Despite his corporal punishment, I was never afraid of Dad. I highly respected him because ours was a loving father-son relationship.

Ultimately, what I remember and treasure the most about Dad was seeing firsthand how the Lord used him in the church and community to improve the quality of life for Christians and non-Christians alike. Without fanfare, Dad's life glorified God because he selflessly and faithfully taught, mentored, and assisted so many people who today enhance the quality of life for people around the world.

Dad taught the preteen boys' Sunday school class at church occasionally, although he was primarily responsible for the adult male class.

All our classes used the predetermined lesson plans (Quarterlies). During the week, he would study Sunday's lesson while sitting in his recliner in our living room. (He used several Bibles, commentaries, and study materials that prepared him well for those speculative or controversial questions that would arise occasionally).

Some Sundays, I'd attend his class to watch him affirm fundamental biblical doctrines and teachings. When class discussions veered off, he would gently lead the students back on track by saying something like: "Yes! You have a point there. But let's see what the Bible says."

Dad also served faithfully as the Chairman of the Board of Deacons for the large, urban, prestigious church we attended. During his tenure, the Senior Pastor died unexpectedly on two separate occasions within a five-year span.

Not only did the Lord use Dad to provide the strong, caring leadership needed for church stability during those two very traumatic periods, but He also used his servant leadership to help maintain peace and tranquility through three diverse pastoral vision and leadership transition periods.

Watching and listening to Dad helped me understand how a "godly man" conducts himself. He would always tell me: "Stay humble, Son." As insightful as always, Dad was teaching me that self-centered motives have no place in the heart of the "godly" leader. Because not only do they hamper our close spiritual relationships with the Lord, they also negate our overall service effectiveness as well. Truly, I can say Dad "*Lived the life*" before me.[1]

Grandma was the gracious "diplomat." I can recall when we lived in the housing projects next door to "Granny." Although we were from vastly different cultures, Grandma invited her to our home for fellowship and an occasional meal.

I learned many wonderful lessons about Christian living from all three parents. But it was Grandma who taught me something I find myself verbally repeating today. Once, I asked her why she treated people with kindness as she had, and her reply was: "It's just nice to be nice!"

I never saw Grandma act reclusive, embittered, or vindictive toward others. Some attributed her gracious manner to her advanced age since she was born in the South shortly after the turn of the last century, but I did not. I attributed it to the refining work the Lord Jesus Christ was doing in her heart after she accepted Him as her personal Lord and Savior when she was about nine years old.

Her remarkable ability to show kindness, even though she was a victim of abuse, was a clear sign the Lord was transforming and refining her. He

---

[1] Dad often shared the story of how the Lord impressed him to: "Live the [Christian] life before this boy," referring to me.

gave Grandma a heart to love and forgive, and this was especially telling in her choice of a favorite Bible verse:

> Come to me, all of you who are weary and carry heavy burdens, and I will give you rest. Take my yoke upon you. Let me teach you, because I am humble and gentle at heart, and you will find rest for your souls. For my yoke is easy to bear, and the burden I give you is light (Matthew 11:28–30 NLT).

The more I watched her express love and forgiveness, whether toward friend or foe, the more I grew to understand what noble Christian living is supposed to look like. For she epitomized Ephesians 4:32 (KJV): "And be ye kind one to another, tenderhearted, forgiving one another, even as God for Christ's sake hath forgiven you."

I greatly miss Mom, Dad, and Grandma, as they have long since gone to be with Jesus. (But I am comforted knowing that someday I will see them again in Heaven. *Amen!*)

They helped to cultivate in me an insatiable appetite for God's Word because I wanted to learn more about the God they were showing and telling me.

I started reading the King James Version since it was the predominant version used in our home and church at that time. Despite its archaic language, I memorized its contents and grew to understand and cherish it over time.

My room was my "hideout," where I would read my Bible for hours at a time. (When I was away from home, I read a miniature Bible that would fit perfectly inside my shirt breast pocket.) It was here where I first read the Parable of the Unforgiving Servant in Matthew 18:21–35:

> Then came Peter to Him, and said, Lord, how oft shall my brother sin against me, and I forgive him? till seven times?
> Jesus saith unto him, I say not unto thee, Until seven times: but, Until seventy times seven.
> Therefore is the kingdom of heaven likened unto a certain king, which would take account of his servants. And when he had begun to reckon, one was brought unto him, which owed him ten thousand talents.
> But forasmuch as he had not to pay, his lord commanded him to be sold, and his wife, and children, and all that he had, and payment to be made. The servant therefore fell down, and worshipped him, saying, Lord, have patience with me, and I will pay thee all. Then the lord of that servant was moved with compassion, and loosed him, and forgave him the debt.

But the same servant went out, and found one of his fellowservants, which owed him an hundred pence: and he laid hands on him, and took him by the throat, saying, Pay me that thou owest. And his fellowservant fell down at his feet, and besought him, saying, Have patience with me, and I will pay thee all. And he would not: but went and cast him into prison, till he should pay the debt.
So when his fellowservants saw what was done, they were very sorry, and came and told unto their lord all that was done. Then his lord, after that he had called him, said unto him, O thou wicked servant, I forgave thee all that debt, because thou desiredst me: Shouldest not thou also have had compassion on thy fellowservant, even as I had pity on thee? And his lord was wroth, and delivered him to the tormentors, till he should pay all that was due unto him.
So likewise shall my heavenly Father do also unto you, if ye from your hearts forgive not every one his brother their trespasses.

My initial impression of the servant was he had his fellow servant imprisoned to get the money he needed to repay his debt. I could not understand why the king was angry with him because if I owed money, I would do what was necessary to collect any outstanding debts.

But as I grew older, it became even clearer the Lord was teaching a profound lesson on forgiveness (verse 33): "Shouldest not thou also have had compassion on thy fellowservant, even as I had pity on thee?"

This was a lesson accompanied by a stern and somber warning (verse 36): "So likewise shall my heavenly Father do also unto you, if ye from your hearts forgive not every one his brother their trespasses."

In other words, the parable's central message is crystal clear: *God forgives us, and He expects us to forgive others in like manner.* Yet, many complex implications emerge from the comparison and contrast of the Forgiving King and the Unforgiving Servant.

This book was written to show the importance of forgiveness in the Christian's life by exploring the comparison and contrast using supporting Scriptures, selective works, and interactive activities. Theological terms will be highlighted in bold italics to aid in further research as needed.

While we await His glorious return, our Lord Jesus Christ expects us to practice radical forgiveness that transforms others and us. *What about you?*

Before presenting Chapter 1, which highlights four lessons Jesus taught His disciples before He tells the parable, I will share an old hymn that features God's radical forgiveness.

There Is a Fountain
William Cowper

There is a fountain filled with blood Drawn from Immanuel's veins, And sinners plunged beneath that flood Lose all their guilty stains: Lose all their guilty stains, Lose all their guilty stains; And sinners plunged beneath that flood Lose all their guilty stains.

The dying thief rejoiced to see That fountain in his day, And there may I, though vile as he, Wash all my sins away: Wash all my sins away, Wash all my sins away; And there may I, though vile as he, Wash all my sins away.

Dear dying Lamb, Thy precious blood Shall never lose its pow'r, Till all the ransomed Church of God Be saved to sin no more: Be saved to sin no more, Be saved to sin no more; Till all the ransomed Church of God Be saved to sin no more.

E'er since by faith I saw the stream Thy flowing wounds supply, Redeeming love has been my theme And shall be till I die: And shall be till I die, And shall be till I die; Redeeming love has been my theme And shall be till I die.

When this poor lisping, stamm'ring tongue Lies silent in the grave, Then in a nobler, sweeter song, I'll sing Thy pow'r to save: I'll sing Thy pow'r to save, I'll sing Thy pow'r to save; Then in a nobler, sweeter song, I'll sing Thy pow'r to save.[2]

---

[2]William Cowper, "There is a Fountain," *101 Hymn Stories*, Kenneth Osbeck, ed., (Grand Rapids: Kregel, 1982) 263.

Chapter One

Chapter 1
Four Important Lessons

If you were in perfect health with all your faculties but only had one year to live, what would be most important to you? How would you reprioritize your life? What would be the last thing you'd want to say or do?

A common response would be to travel to some exotic place, spend quality time with family and friends, or to pursue some unfinished personal endeavor.

Not so with Jesus. He knew He would die on the cross within about a year's time. Yet He spent His remaining days training His disciples through four lessons about the Kingdom of God.

Lesson One: Who Am I?

In Matthew 16:13–18 (NIV), the Lord and His disciples are in Galilee near Caesarea Philippi. There, He asks: "Who do people say the Son of Man is?"

His disciples' responses were varied: "Some say that you are John the Baptist; others say you are Elijah; still others say that you are Jeremiah or one of the prophets."

Not concerned with public opinion, Jesus asks two more personal questions: *"But what about you?"* he asked. *"Who do you say I am?"*

Peter's response, although impulsive, revealed his present understanding of Jesus: "You are the Christ (the Anointed One, the Messiah) the Son of the Living God!" With that, the Lord replied:

> "Blessed are you, Simon son of Jonah, for this was not revealed to you by flesh and blood, but by my Father in heaven. And I tell you that you are Peter, and on this rock I will build my church, and the gates of Hades will not overcome it" (Matthew 16:17–18 NIV).

I am glad Jesus Christ is never concerned about satisfying the public's opinion regarding His identity. Even today, some refer to Him as a prophet or a great teacher; others say He was a good man who died a horrible death on a cross.

In my life, I've heard responses to the "Who is Jesus?" question in the form of another question: "How can you believe in some dead man's religion?"

Those who ask this question are looking through a prism that views Jesus only as the *Son of Man*, who died on the cross one tragic Friday afternoon.

But if death were all there was to know about Jesus Christ; then as it reads in 1 Corinthians 15:19 (KJV), we would be: *"most miserable!"*

But death is <u>not</u> the end. There is the Christ, the **Son of God**, who arose on that glorious Sunday morning leaving us with an empty tomb. We need to acknowledge this historical event as well.

When we consider both (i.e., Jesus' death and resurrection) equally and objectively, everything about Jesus Christ as the God-man becomes crystal clear. Josh McDowell writes:

> If God did become man, who or what would He be like? He would possess the attributes of God, He would have an unusual entrance into this world, He would perform feats of the supernatural, He would be sinless; a lasting and universal impression would be left by Him...God came to earth in the person of Jesus Christ, and in Jesus we see manifest the attributes of God and the characteristics that would accompany a God-man.[3]

Like Peter, we too understand and acknowledge Jesus Christ is more than just a person who

---

[3]Josh McDowell, *Evidence that Demands a Verdict*, rev. ed., vol. 1, (San Bernardino: Here's Life Publishers, Inc., 1979) 111.

suffered a tragic death on a cross because we know Him as our:

> Advocate, Alpha and Omega, Bread of Life, Bridegroom, Christ, Deliverer, Faithful and True, Friend, Good Shepherd, Great God, Great Physician, High Priest, Immanuel, Intercessor, King of Glory, King of Kings, Lamb of God, Light of the World, Lion of Judah, Lord, Lover of Our Soul, Mighty God, Mediator, Messiah, Prince of Peace, Redeemer, Resurrection and Life, Righteous Judge, Rock and Fortress, Savior, True Prophet, The Truth, The Way, and The Word.

Isn't it amazing how God is not too big to care for each of us individually? He is **omniscient**, having "all knowledge" of every detail of our lives including the exact number of hairs on our heads (Matthew 10:30).

Yet He is small enough to care for us personally by asking each of us the question: "Who do _you_ say I am?" Ultimately, He wants to resolve our false assumptions and presuppositions so that He can establish an intimacy with us that lasts forever.

After Peter's response, the Lord foretells of His death to prepare His disciples for His departure. Given Peter's verbal objection, a second lesson was sorely needed.

Lesson Two: Listen To Him!

In Matthew 17:1–9, the Lord takes Peter, James, and John up a high mountain where He was "transfigured" (Greek: *metamorpho*) or transformed before them.[4] Jesus' face and clothing turned bright as the sun, and Moses and Elijah appeared suddenly, talking to Him about what would happen at Jerusalem.

Out of fear and not knowing what to say, Peter interrupts by saying three temporary dwellings for the Lord and His two esteemed guests could be built. But while He was speaking, a cloud overshadowed them, and a voice said: "This is my beloved Son, in whom I am well pleased. Listen to Him!" (v. 5).

Matthew's account of this event has always fascinated me because, at first glance, we could almost miss the command: *"Listen to Him!"* But these words capture the essence of the Lord's earthly ministry as Everett F. Harrison notes:

> Clearly Peter was being subjected to censure...Whether he realized it or not, Peter was ostensibly putting Jesus on the same plane with these Old Testament servants of God ("one for you and one for Moses and one for Elijah"). That will not

---

[4]James Strong, "μεταμορφόω," *A Concise Dictionary of the Words in the Greek New Testament,* in *The Exhaustive Concordance of the Bible,* (Iowa Falls: Riverside, 1980?) 47.

do. God spoke in the past to the fathers through the prophets, but now He has spoken through a *Son*. The difference must be understood and respected. Jesus is a prophet but more than a prophet.[5]

No other person in history has received the accolades our Lord Jesus Christ receives here.

It is also worth noting the voice declared He was the "Beloved Son" of God in human flesh. But, the proclamation did not stop at declaring Jesus' deity. It also implied His words were "greater" than those of Moses the Lawgiver, and Elijah the Prophet.

Such a statement was preposterous at the time, given that God spoke to Moses "face to face" as He would to a friend (Exodus 33:11, Numbers 12:8), and Elijah was considered the Prophet of God (1 Kings 17:24, Luke 1:17).

Parenthetically, we should note Jesus was not concerned with achieving "celebrity status" or how He was ranked. Even after such a magnanimous proclamation, He maintains His humble demeanor, which speaks volumes about His character and the absence of ulterior motives.

---

[5]Everett F. Harrison, *A Short Life of Christ*, reprint, (Grand Rapids: Wm. B. Eerdmans, 2001) 159.

Consequently, Jesus taught that He did not come to destroy the Mosaic Law or invalidate Elijah and the prophets. He came to fulfill them (Matthew 5:17). In this way, He <u>always</u> affirmed the importance of those holy men who preceded him.

Going back to the question about a "dead man's religion" for a moment. I <u>can</u> believe in Jesus Christ (because of the historical fact of the empty tomb and) because the voice heard here affirms His ***Pre-incarnate Deity***.

After rejoining the other disciples, Jesus goes on to settle a petty dispute about Kingdom status in His third lesson.

Lesson Three: Who Is The Greatest?

Matthew 18:1–4 takes place at Capernaum. There, the disciples ask: "Who is going to be the greatest in the Kingdom of Heaven?" Here, the Lord shows great patience as they struggled to understand the importance of humility, selflessness, and forbearance. One author writes:

> How His disciples must have saddened Him as they disputed among themselves as to who should be the greatest under the Messiah's reign...Entrance into God's kingdom requires the trusting humility of a child. Growth in the kingdom involves childlike obedience, faith, selflessness, and love—the essence of Christian

> discipleship...Service to others, as opposed to self-seeking, gives the highest claim to honor.[6]

To answer their question, the Lord places a child in their midst and says:

> I tell you the truth, unless you turn from your sins and become like little children, you will never get into the Kingdom of Heaven. So anyone who becomes as humble as this little child is the greatest in the Kingdom of Heaven (Matthew 18:3–4 NLT).

For the better part of three years, the Lord has been teaching His disciples about humility and self-denial: "If any man will come after me, let him deny himself, and take up his cross, and follow me" (Matthew 16:24 KJV). Yet they still did not understand.

Moreover, they had the Lord as their prime example of humility and self-sacrifice. He freely emptied Himself of His deity and took on a human form so that He could offer Himself as our payment for sin.

The disciples had not yet understood the Kingdom is spiritual, not physical. Although it is invisible

---

[6]Ray F. Robbins, *The Life and Ministry of Our Lord*, (Nashville: Convention Press, 1970) 106.

now, it will be visible soon. There, our Lord reigns in His full majesty, and there, flesh, blood, sin, selfishness, and Satan are excluded forever (1 Corinthians 6:9–10).

As it was two thousand years ago, it is still true today. We live in a worldly kingdom that prefers retaliation over reconciliation. Even from the age of a young child, we are taught not to let anyone "take advantage" of us or "show any weakness."

The Lord characterized the *End Times* as a period of escalating hostility. We see overt *"Signs of the Times"* in heightened levels of national and international warfare. But we see more subtle signs in the proliferation of random assaults, terrorist attacks, school violence, workplace violence, and road rage.

Although tragic, these events are mere byproducts of a violent, "dog-eat-dog" world where "only the strong survive," and the "ends always justify the means." Because "it's never personal; it's only business."

To turn His disciples from such worldly standards, the Lord introduces them to Kingdom living that transcends through His fourth lesson: forgiveness.

Lesson Four: Seventy Times Seven

In Matthew 18:21–22, it was only "natural" for Peter to ask the question: How often should I forgive? Seven times? From our human perspective, forgiving once is remarkable, and forgiving seven times is extraordinary.

Often, we keep track of the times when someone offends us, and we bear grudges against those who have offended us when we should overlook the offense and forgive the offender.

We also "rate" sins on a "sliding scale" as though one sin was more heinous than another. But we can't make such comparisons since <u>all</u> of us have sinned, and we are deficient of God's righteous standards (Romans 3:23).

Rating sin can lead to falsely characterizing others for past criminal behavior, drug use, marital infidelity, divorce, or an abhorrent lifestyle—even when they now live for Christ fully.

Moreover, it's hypocritical to condemn someone for his or her past when we have "skeletons" in our closet, as Jesus says in Matthew 7:3–5 (NLT):

> And why worry about a speck in your friend's eye when you have a log in your own? How can you think of saying to your friend, "Let me help you get rid of that speck in your eye," when you can't see past the log in your own eye? Hypocrite! First get rid of the log in your

own eye; then you will see well enough to deal with the speck in your friend's eye.

Our "sliding scales" have to be challenged. We cannot impose human standards on godly principles by forgiving certain offenses or forgiving only to a certain level.

The Lord's response was immediate: *Not just seven times, but seventy times seven!*

In other words, we must be perfect, even as our Heavenly Father is perfect (Matthew 5:48) by forgiving to the extent that He has forgiven us.

Thus we do not seek to avenge, harbor grudges, or express ill will toward those people who may have wronged us. Instead, we give them a "clean slate" and treat them as if they have never wronged us — just as He did for us.

This expands on the Lord's Kingdom principles He expresses in His **Model Prayer**:

> And forgive us our debts, as we also have forgiven our debtors...For if you forgive other people when they sin against you, your heavenly Father will also forgive you. But if you do not forgive others their sins, your Father will not forgive your sins" (Matthew 6:12–14 NIV).

Citing from Deuteronomy 32:35 and Proverbs 25:21–22, the apostle Paul expounds on these ideas in his letter to the church at Rome:

> Dear friends, never take revenge. Leave that to the righteous anger of God. For the Scriptures say, "I will take revenge; I will pay them back," says the LORD. Instead, "If your enemies are hungry, feed them. If they are thirsty, give them something to drink. In doing this, you will heap burning coals of shame on their heads." Don't let evil conquer you, but conquer evil by doing good (Romans 12:19–21 NLT).

While growing up, I remember hearing my parents, teachers, and ministers say: "God hates the sin, but He loves the sinner." Over time, I grew to understand the meaning of these words: the Lord makes a clear distinction between the offense (sin) and the offender (sinner).

We are imperfect human beings fully capable of sinning and constantly need forgiveness. To illustrate this point, the Lord contrasts the Forgiving King with the Unforgiving Servant. I will present the Forgiving King in the next chapter.

Before moving to the next chapter, I will introduce two fictional characters: John and Joanne, who will experience radical forgiveness themselves.

John and Joanne were from the same city and had known each other for years. John was a local area native, while Joanne's family moved there just before she attended middle school.

They were attracted to each other in high school. There, John was the captain of the varsity football team, and Joanne was on the cheerleading squad.

When they met through a mutual friend, it was like magic; they talked for hours about their love for the Lord, the college they wanted to attend, where they wanted to live, getting married, and raising a family.

They discovered they had very similar interests. Shortly after graduation, John proposed and they were married at the small church they both attended.

The pastor was like a second father to John. He helped him decide which of the four major colleges he should attend. As it turned out, they chose the same college.

John received a full athletic scholarship, and Joanne received an academic scholarship. While in college, they were very active at the church their pastor suggested they attend.

By the end of their senior year, their future looked bright. John was an All-American Heisman Candidate, and Joanne was a busy mother, wife, and homemaker with a third child on the way; this young family was growing and prospering.

Chapter Two

Chapter 2
The Forgiving King

In Matthew 18:23–35, Jesus Christ, our Master Teacher, uses poignant imagery to illustrate how true forgiveness should work. The Lord was extremely adept at using such visuals, as Bill Austin observes:

> All that Jesus taught by word and example was to enlist men [and women] into a relationship with God which would acknowledge His sovereignty and kingship. The kingdom of God is His domain, the sphere of His reign and rule. While Jesus obviously anticipated the future glory of the kingdom, He also insisted that kingdom principles could begin immediately with a relationship of obedience to God. His parables, therefore, were often urgent appeals for men [and women] to prepare for the future kingdom by knowing and serving the King in the present. [7]

To better appreciate the Forgiving King's actions, let's take a brief look at a massive forgiven debt.

---

[7] Bill R. Austin, *Austin's Topical History of Christianity,* (Wheaton: Tyndale House, 1983) 34.

A Massive Debt Is Forgiven

The parable begins with an ancient monarch reckoning with his servants. Although all the servants were equally accountable, one is brought before him owing ten thousand talents.

The talent was the largest measurement for precious and non-precious metals for the Jews. Its weight ranged anywhere from 90 to 120 pounds, (or what a "normal man" could carry), and it represented the wages a common person earned over a "lifetime."

At the time He spoke this parable, the value of a talent was worth somewhere between $1,000.00 and $1,500.00 in today's US dollars. Multiply this by ten thousand, and we have a debt ranging between $10 and $15 million.

As with Joseph in the *Old Testament*, it was common for servants to have responsibilities that extended beyond menial chores since they were of greater value than common laborers.

Many worked as stewards, clerks, teachers, physicians, skilled artisans, accountants, and overseers of the owner's farm, household, and business.

Not all servants were honest, however. Some resorted to trickery to embezzle large sums of money from their owner's estate.

The parable makes no mention of how the debt was incurred. But as an integral part of his master's household, the servant could have incurred it through fraudulent transactions while acting on his master's behalf.[8]

The servant was guilty of mismanagement by being solely responsible for a massive debt, and the Forgiving King was well within his rights to order the servant and his family to be imprisoned and/or his property seized until the entire debt was repaid.

The servant had nothing to bargain with. He owned nothing that would satisfy a debt that would have taken him several lifetimes to repay. In addition, the likelihood of him repaying the debt from prison was utterly impossible.

Before the officials could imprison the guilty servant, he falls on his knees and begs for mercy: "Be patient with me, and I will pay you back!" (Matthew 18:29)

---

[8]See: Merrill C. Tenney, *New Testament Survey*, 16th printing, (Grand Rapids: Wm. B. Eerdmans, 1980) 49–50; Joachim, Jeremias, *Jerusalem in the Time of Jesus*, 3rd ed., trans. F.H. and C.H. Cave, (Philadelphia: Fortress, 1969) 345–351; Cecil B. Murphey, Comp., *The Dictionary of Biblical Literacy*, (Nashville: Oliver-Nelson, 1989) 362; and James M. Freeman, "Elevation Of Slaves," reprint, in *Manners and Customs of the Bible*, (Plainfield: Logos Intl., 1972) 47.

Then the Forgiving King does something extraordinary. Not moved with rage or vengeance, he "was moved with compassion" to extend unmerited favor (***Grace***) toward a debtor in desperate need of complete forgiveness, as one writer notes:

> In the parable of the unforgiving slave (18:23–35), the first slave owes the king ten thousand talents (v. 24)...Given the enormity of his debt, the slave's promise to repay everything is absurd (v. 26). The king does not merely postpone or reduce the debt—he cancels it.[9]

In this parable, God is the Forgiving King who loves and forgives us in a way far beyond our ability to comprehend. We often take for granted the enormity of our sin debt, which has been forgiven, forgotten, and canceled through the redemptive work of Christ.

Why We Need Forgiveness

Sometimes, we forget how we have offended God and others. We've needed God's forgiveness from the beginning: when He created everything and it was very good.

---

[9] J. Knox Chamblin, "Matthew," *Baker Commentary on the Bible*, 5th printing, ed. Walter A. Elwell, (Grand Rapids: Baker, 2008) 745.

God told Adam that he was free to eat the fruit from every tree in the garden except the Tree of the Knowledge of Good and Evil. The moment he ate that fruit, he would die.

Adam and Eve disobeyed God and ate the fruit. As result, spiritual and physical death happened just as God warned. Physical death came gradually, as Adam lived to be 930 years old. However, spiritual death (*The Fall*) happened instantly, as sin was introduced into the world to taint God's perfect creation.

Original Sin was transmitted to all as descendants of Adam and Eve (Genesis 2:16-17; 3:6-19). As a result, we are born with an internal condition (*Fallen Nature*) that causes us to think, speak, and act in a depraved manner. Thus, we are sinners, not because of our sinful behavior but because of the Fallen Nature we've inherited from our ancestors, which is at work inside of us to produce sinful behavior.

In other words, as our ancestors chose to sin, we tend to choose to worship other gods, create idols, use God's name irreverently, break the Sabbath, disrespect our parents, commit murder, be sexually promiscuous, steal, lie, and covet. (We fail miserably at keeping just the Ten Commandments. Imagine how frustrated we would be trying to keep all 613 statutes of the *Old Testament Law*).

So when a quiet, delicate, unassuming, "good person" practices "shocking" sinful behavior, they are being true to their fallen nature. This is why the Bible rightly teaches that all have sinned (Romans 5:12).

As fig leaves were an inadequate covering for Adam and Eve's shame and nakedness, so are our "good deeds" inadequate to please God since they are sin-tainted. As such, they do not impress God, nor do they influence His favor. He calls them what they are: "Filthy rags" (Isaiah 64:6).

God is fully qualified to make this distinction because He never fell from perfection; we did, and we've lost fellowship with Him forever as a result. By nature, we are morally and spiritually unfit to occupy His holy, glorious heaven, and we are well-suited to occupy a sinful, tormenting hell.

We've all missed God's mark, and whether we consider the miss to be one-quarter of an inch or one million miles—it's irrelevant because WE <u>ALL</u> <u>HAVE MISSED THE MARK!</u>

We can never be "good" enough to earn God's righteousness because our external, physical efforts cannot fix our fallen nature. Even with all the technology and self-help resources we have at our disposal, we can do nothing to correct our sinful condition.

We see the utter futility of those who try to use wealth, sports notoriety, political power, corporate achievement, social status, academia, technology, and medicine to alleviate their sin problem, yet to no avail.

Ultimately, we are helpless and hopeless without God's intervention through radical forgiveness.

Here, beyond mere sympathy, God shows empathy toward us when He cancels our unpayable debt forever.

Our Debt Is Canceled Forever

Like the servant, we are encumbered with a massive debt far beyond our ability to repay — *sin!* Yet God graciously provides His remedy as promised in Leviticus 17:11 (KJV):

> For the life of the flesh is in the blood: and I have given it to you upon the altar to make an atonement for your souls: for it is the blood that maketh an atonement for the soul.

God fixed our sin problem when He became human (*Incarnation*) in the person of Jesus Christ. The apostle John writes:

> And the Word was made flesh, and dwelt among us, and we beheld His glory, the

> glory as of the only begotten of the Father, full of grace and truth (John 1:14 KJV).

The Lord canceled our sin debt and restored our lost fellowship by using His sinless life and precious blood, as Hebrews 9:11–12 (KJV) teaches:

> But Christ being come an high priest of good things to come, by a greater and more perfect tabernacle, not made with hands, that is to say, not of this building; Neither by the blood of goats and calves, but by His own blood He entered in once into the holy place, having obtained eternal redemption for us.

Guilty, broken, and ashamed for his blunder, the servant cries out for mercy.

But, the Forgiving King does not define his servant by his blunder. Instead, he looks beyond the debt to consider what was best for all by extending exceptional grace and mercy.

Here, he sees a person needing dignity and restoration, as did the father seeing his son in the parable of the Prodigal Son in Luke 15:11-32 (NLT). In both instances, the focus was not on the offense. The focus was on reconciling with someone who: "was dead and is alive again; he was lost and is found!"

With the debt canceled, the servant was permitted to continue conducting transactions on his master's behalf. One writer makes this observation:

> The order is given that the debtor be sold, with all he has…touched with pity…the king decides on a magnanimous policy…two benefits conferred; set free from imprisonment, debt absolutely canceled, not merely time given for payment. A third benefit implied, continuance in office.[10]

Our massive, unpayable sin debt has been forgiven and canceled forever through the blood of Jesus Christ. But even more extraordinary is how favorably we are treated beyond our restoration. Before exploring this in the next chapter, let's continue John and Joanne's story.

> John won the Heisman Trophy and became the first pick in the NFL Draft. As it turned out, the team that selected him was only fifty miles from his hometown.
>
> At the recommendation of certain college teammates, John hired an agent who

---

[10]Alexander Balmain Bruce, "The Synoptic Gospels," *The Expositor's Greek New Testament*, vol. 1, reprint, ed., Robertson Nicholl, (Grand Rapids: Wm. B. Eerdmans, 1980) 242.

negotiated his contracts and handled his personal banking accounts.

With the money from the first rookie contract, John purchased a home and became a hometown celebrity.

As time passed, two other contracts were negotiated so that by his seventh year, John was the highest paid player in the NFL.

More years pass; John achieved All-Pro status while Joanne was busy homeschooling the kids and performing many church and community functions.

When the children started their teen years, John and Joanne decided to open a $50,000 college fund for each child.

They decided to meet with the branch manager to set up the accounts.

Chapter Three

Chapter 3
The Servant Is Restored

Our Forgiving King's grace and mercy yield five awards that greatly benefit us today.

First Award: A New Spiritual Being

In John 3:3, we read how through the *Second Birth* or *New Birth*,[11] the fallen nature we acquired at birth is transformed spiritually.

As we invite Jesus Christ into our lives by faith, we receive a new internal being that helps us perform God's will and secure His favor.

No longer spiritually dead, God's Holy Spirit now lives inside us, and He transforms us into "new" creatures (1 Corinthians 5:17). Thus, the old nature, which was spiritually dead, is brought to life by a new life that desires to follow Christ.

---

[11]*"Second Birth," "New Birth," "In Christ," "Born Again,"* and *"Union with Christ"* are synonymous terms that refer to a spiritual process that has both human and divine elements. The human element (*Conversion*) is when we reach out to Jesus Christ with sincere repentance and faith. The divine element (*Regeneration*) is when God's Holy Spirit inhabits us forever and awakens (*Quickens*) our spirits simultaneously.

We may not experience any significant external changes. Yet we have a new, internal spiritual being that makes us acceptable before God as James Madison Pendleton writes:

> Regeneration involves the illumination of the understanding, the consecration of the affections, and the rectification of the will. To use Paul's language, 'Ye were once darkness, but now are ye light in the Lord,' Ephesians v. 8.[12]

God is no respecter of persons, and access to His kingdom is by spiritual, not material means. Human supremacy is our chief aim, while God wants to transform our hearts. Once this happens, everything else we have will become His property.

With our new spiritual nature comes a new standing before God, and this is our second award.

Second Award: God Declares Us Righteous

By faith, we have a new position in Christ where God exchanges Jesus' sinless life for our sinful life (***Justification***). Now, when God looks at us, He does not see us as vile sinners.

---

[12] J. M. Pendleton, *Christian Doctrines*, 33rd printing, (Valley Forge: Judson, 1976) 59.

He sees His sinless Son, Jesus Christ the Righteous One, suitable for eternal fellowship, as Isaiah writes:

> But He was wounded for our transgressions, He was bruised for our iniquities: the chastisement of our peace was upon him; and with His stripes we are healed (Isaiah 53:5 KJV).

Like condemned criminals standing before a judge about to sentence us to death, we stand before the Forgiving King of the universe, guilty of the nature we've inherited and the sins we've committed.

Guilty, condemned, helpless, and hopeless. Yet, at the last instant, His Son steps forward to assume our sin, guilt, and penalty, while we assume His innocence, righteousness, and glory. Now, instead of sentencing us to death, which is proper and just, the Judge releases us with a new identity, having expunged our record.

Jesus Christ died on our behalf at Calvary because He loves us more than we could ever comprehend. It is not our works but our faith in His *work* that secures our new position and eternal fellowship.

In Romans 5 (the *Justification Chapter*), Paul writes how we were separated from God. But we are now reconciled to God through the blood of

Jesus Christ. Once enemies, we are now at peace with him. This is God's grace, and it is amazing.

When the good news of Jesus Christ reaches good soil, it produces good fruit. Having secured our being and position forever, the Lord empowers us to live lives that honor Him. This captures the essence of our third award.

Third Award: We Have God's Spirit inside Us

Before leaving, the Lord promised the Spirit would abide with us and be inside us.

> And I will ask the Father, and He will give you another Advocate who will never leave you. He is the Holy Spirit, who leads into all truth. The world cannot receive him, because it isn't looking for Him and doesn't recognize him. But you know him, because He lives with you now and later will be in you. No, I will not abandon you as orphans—I will come to you (John 14:16–18 NLT).

The Holy Spirit molds our thoughts, words, and actions into Christ's likeness (***Sanctification***) just as He promises:

> Ye are the light of the world. A city that is set on an hill cannot be hid. Neither do men [or women] light a candle, and put it under a bushel, but on a candlestick; and

it giveth light unto all that are in the house. Let your light so shine before men [and women], that they may see your good works, and glorify your Father which is in heaven (Matthew 5:14–16 KJV).

Forgiven and restored, God gives us the power to "grow up" morally and spiritually. Our works are never performed to achieve *Salvation*. We work because the Spirit inside us constrains us to make godly, moral choices and perform selfless, noble acts, as Augustus H. Strong writes:

> That in this conflict the Holy Spirit enables the Christian, through increasing faith, more fully and consciously to appropriate Christ, and thus progressively to make a conquest of the remaining sinfulness of his [or her] nature.[13]

Romans 12:2 (KJV) reads: "And be not conformed to this world: but be ye transformed by the renewing of your mind, that ye may prove what is that good, and acceptable, and perfect, will of God."

With a renewed, willing mind, God gives us a progressive yearning for godly things like reading His Word, praying, worshipping, fellowshipping,

---

[13]Augustus H. Strong, *Systematic Theology*, 31st printing, (Valley Forge: Judson, 1976) 870.

and serving others. Simultaneously, He develops within us a growing disdain for worldly things that stunt our spiritual growth and hinder our fellowship with God.

Although we walk in the Spirit by trusting in, surrendering to, and serving our Lord, we will never achieve perfection in this life relying on our strength alone.

Yet, Jesus Christ makes intercession for us when we grieve the Holy Spirit by walking in sin and not in the Spirit. We can disobey or rebel against the Lord out of pride, selfishness, or spite like children having temper tantrums.

But like the Prodigal Son, we "come to ourselves" by turning from our sin and returning to the Lord, mindful of what He did for us at Calvary. Here, we rely on the Lord to strengthen us so that we do not repeat the same sins.

In essence, we grow to understand that although we are imperfect humans, we cannot please the Lord by pursuing sin and selfishness at the same time.

Our imperfection does not signal our defeat. It only reminds us how far from Christ's perfection we are and of how we must rely on His Holy Spirit to help us grow stronger each day.

Jesus Christ was the only perfect example, and He can help us live a life of moral and spiritual excellence that contrasts our former life of sin.

As Jeremiah and Paul so aptly observe, boasting is never directed toward our feeble works. We should always point toward the Lord who is at work inside us (Jeremiah 9:24, 1 Corinthians 1:31).

Our total perfection has been promised to happen when the Kingdom of God is fully revealed (1 Corinthians 15:50). Then we will experience the pinnacle of God's redemptive work where the wicked cease from troubling, and the weary are at rest (Job 3:17). This is our fourth award.

Fourth Award: We Have Eternal Fellowship with God

When the Lord returns, we will have immortal bodies capable of experiencing God's glory and majesty forever (*Glorification*). Of this glorious transformation, Paul writes:

> So when this corruptible shall have put on incorruption, and this mortal shall have put on immortality, then shall be brought to pass the saying that is written, Death is swallowed up in victory (1 Corinthians 15:54 KJV).

In this blessed eternal state, we will experience unbroken, untainted fellowship with our holy God and see him "as He is" because we will be "like him" (1 John 3:2 KJV).

We read in James 4:6 that God resists the proud and gives grace to the humble. Jesus Christ is both Lord and Savior, and those who choose not to acknowledge Him in this life will face Him as Eternal Judge in the next.

For those of us who love Him, and whose faith begins and ends with Him, He is our hope, peace, expectation, and great reward — now and forever.

In the meantime, unlimited access to God has been restored. This is our fifth award.

Fifth Award: Our Access Is Restored

This world often demands continual payment for our offenses while our Forgiving King does not. He keeps no record of our debt. Nor does He impose a probation period until we "prove ourselves."

He restores us to full access to His Kingdom without restriction. In 1 John 4:10, love is defined by how God loved us enough to send His Son to be the ransom payment for our sin. It is only through this unselfish love that we can be restored.

Ultimately, Jesus Christ left His deity and glory, not because of what we could do for Him but because we needed Him to pay our debt of sin at Calvary.

Because of the efficacy of Jesus' immeasurable work, even those who have yet to believe in Him; His is the only hope for restoration, as He yet declares today: "The time is fulfilled, and the kingdom of God is at hand" (Mark 1:15 KJV).

His is the greatest of all proclamations, because with it, He heralds a *New Testament* age for everyone everywhere that revokes our claims of neutrality toward God.

For when we repent (turn from sin) and believe the gospel (turn to God through Christ), God cancels our sin debt and restores us immediately. There is the one caveat to this access, found in John 8:24, where the Lord warns that all those who do not believe in Him will die in their sins.

Thus, we can either choose to receive His gift of restoration on earth plus eternal life in heaven, or we can reject it and be separated from Him in this life and face a tormented hell in the next.

Concerning our restored fellowship that Jesus freely provides for us, the apostle John writes:

> Yet to all who did receive him, to those who believed in His name, He gave the right to become children of God—children born not of natural descent, nor of human

decision or a husband's will, but born of God (John 1:12–13 NIV).

Jesus also says this about His redemptive mission:

> For God so loved the world that He gave His one and only Son, that whoever believes in Him shall not perish but have eternal life. For God did not send His Son into the world to condemn the world, but to save the world through Him (John 3:16–17 NIV).

God directs His children's steps, and He takes special delight in every detail as King David observes in Psalm 37:23. No longer bound by our troubled past, we are fully aware that we matter to God.

Have we arrived yet? Unfortunately, no. Like the Unforgiving Servant, there are those who are unwilling to forgive even the slightest infraction of others. Apparently, these people do not see how our restoration enhances our interpersonal relationships.

Before we look at the Unforgiving Servant in the next chapter, we will continue John and Joanne's story here.

> As John and Joanne tried to transfer money into the college funds, they were shocked to discover they had less than

$50,000 in all their bank accounts combined.

"There has to be some mistake!" John yelled. "I just signed a $15 million contract extension last month! Where did all my money go?"

John and Joanne sat in disbelief as the branch manager showed them copies of documents with John's signature that authorized the agent to act as his power of attorney.

The agent had been taking money for many years and had withdrawn $15 million two weeks earlier.

Chapter Four

Chapter 4
The Unforgiving Servant

Immediately after the Unforgiving Servant left the king, he met another servant who owed him 100 denarii.

The denarius was the most basic unit of Roman coinage and equaled a normal day's wage of approximately sixteen or seventeen cents in today's US money.[14] When multiplied by one hundred, we have a minuscule debt totaling no more than about seventeen dollars.

Compared to the massive debt forgiven, this minuscule debt could have been easily forgiven — and forgotten. But instead, the Unforgiving Servant explodes in anger and assaults his fellow servant by grabbing him by the throat, violently choking him, and yelling: *"Pay me what you owe me!"* (Matthew 18:28)

Here, the unfortunate fellow servant acknowledges his debt, and he begs for mercy: "Have patience with me and I will repay you!" Although both servants made similar requests for mercy, there were two vastly different outcomes.

---

[14] See: Cecil B. Murphey, comp. *The Dictionary of Biblical Literacy*, (Nashville: Thomas Nelson, 1989) 342, Merrill T. Gilbertson, *The Way it was in Bible Times*, Minneapolis, Augsburg, 1959) 118.

Whereas the Unforgiving Servant was forgiven for a $15 million debt; the fellow servant was not forgiven for a debt that was less than twenty dollars. To put his cruelty in perspective, one author makes this observation:

> The second slave owes the first only a hundred denarii, that is, a few dollars; yet the latter responds in utter ruthlessness (vv. 28–30).[15]

One might think, as had I initially, that appropriate force was applied to secure an outstanding debt. But this was not the case. Understanding and compassion were warranted here since both men had a debt beyond their ability to pay, and the likelihood of paying off the debt from prison was a remote possibility.

The Unforgiving Servant prospered from the Forgiving King's graciousness. Yet he showed excessive ruthlessness toward his equal—*a fellow servant who was in need of forgiveness!* The Unforgiving Servant refused to acknowledge that as equals, we share these five characteristics.

We Are Equal Debtors

The Unforgiving Servant failed to realize God created us to inhabit the earth as equals. And since we've all missed the mark, as we studied in

---

[15]Chamblin, 745.

Chapter 2, we are debtors to God and to each other equally by default.

We are guilty of committing sinful acts against God or each other, either directly by commission or indirectly by omission. In other words, none of us are "perfect" enough to encumber another person (or race) with the debt of unforgiveness because all of us are offenders whether we share the same culture, color, or language.

I am saddened by what seems to be heightening racial hostility in the US where civility and understanding should be expressed. I am a natural-born US citizen, and when I consider my history and that of my foreparents, there are those unfortunate issues and associated events, (i.e., slavery, prejudice, segregation, discrimination, etc.) that yet evoke rage from many of my people even today.

Although some feelings of rage may be justified, over the years, I have come to realize that ours is *not* a perfect world. Exploitation and victimization happen everywhere around the globe, leaving me with the realization there is much work to be done everywhere — even within my race.

I must be willing to accept that one particular race did not "corner the market" on victimization or being victimized. There were other races: Native American, Asian, Pacific Islander, Irish, Italian,

Hispanic, etc., that have faced discrimination, injustice, and hostility in this country as well.

Nevertheless, I am most grateful to the Lord to live in this country, which He has greatly blessed with many opportunities we often take for granted: to freely worship, to express opinions without censorship, to elect our representation, and to travel where we want when we want. We also benefit from a capitalistic system that supplies us with goods and services that enhance our standard of living and improve our overall quality of life.

Our sin nature will ensure we will have injustice as long as we live on earth. But as forgiven followers of Jesus Christ, *we are called to exhibit a <u>higher</u> level of spiritual and moral acumen*; one that accepts and embraces others so that we can enhance and preserve civil society.

Thus, as a Christian, I have to acknowledge God created us to help and support each other. Otherwise, our alternative is repression, anarchy, hostility, and more senseless violence.

We Help and Support Each Other

As equals, we can honor and prefer one another as Paul taught in Romans 12:10. In this way, we also give to our Lord, who said, "Inasmuch as ye have done it unto one of the least of these my brethren [and my sisters], ye have done it unto me" (Matthew 25:40 KJV).

We provide aid through food pantries, benevolent funds, and other acts of kindness that allow us to help others in need in tangible and meaningful ways. Then we can affirm we are extensions of God's loving and caring hands.

As recipients, we are charged not to exploit the giver's generosity by deceiving him or her. The Lord will severely punish those who exploit His precious children.

Supporting high-risk behavior constitutes very poor stewardship. It would be better to refer the person who is struggling with an addiction to an appropriate church recovery ministry, Christian nonprofit, counseling service, or social service agency better suited to address his or her most acute need(s).

We can also provide the emotional and spiritual support needed during periods of crisis to show we are a caring community of faith. We pray, provide a listening ear, a shoulder to cry on, a pat on the back, and advice or counsel as givers of supportive care when needed.

Never stockpiling ammunition for gossip, we keep confidences safe and ask for permission to share with professionals who can address the issue(s).[16]

We Have Cordial, Meaningful Relationships

Having been given a "second chance" through faith in Jesus Christ, we can share meaningful fellowships (Greek: *koinonia*) with our equals that dispel disharmony, hatred, and ill will.[17]

We show it is possible for people to coexist peacefully in spite of our differences. This is our distinct Christian witness that verifies our genuine fellowship with God and is seen whenever we meet other Christians who may not share our race, culture, or language, yet we are attracted to them almost instantly and feel comfortable around them, having never met them before.

We share the same Lord, Jesus Christ, and His Spirit within us makes us one, just as He is one with His father as the apostle Paul teaches here:

> Always be humble and gentle. Be patient with each other, making allowance for each other's faults because of your love. Make every effort to keep yourselves

---

[16]We are always "duty bound" to report criminal behavior or warn of hazards that endanger public safety.

[17]Spiros Zodhiates, et al., ed., "κοινωνία," *The Complete Word Study New Testament*, rev. ed., (Chattanooga: AMG, 1992) 873.

united in the Spirit, binding yourselves together with peace. For there is one body and one Spirit, just as you have been called to one glorious hope for the future. There is one Lord, one faith, one baptism, and one God and Father, who is over all and in all and living through all (Ephesians 4:2–6 NLT).

With love and forgiveness, we can contrast the snobbery and prejudice the world accepts and embraces.

The miracle of our Christian synergy validates God's grace in a cold, cruel, and lonely world where smiles are rare, and people are too busy to establish and maintain connections.

We yearn for such opportunities and enjoy fellowship with our brothers and sisters in Christ as we share Sunday dinners after church, celebrate birthdays, wedding anniversaries, and other special occasions.

We also share retreats, picnics, and other events of mutual interest to show the world we are a family where no one is a stranger or an outcast.

Jesus Christ is "a friend who sticks closer than a brother" does (Proverbs 18:24 NIV), and He has equipped us to care for our Christian brothers and sisters everywhere. Although we may disagree about dogma or our form of worship, we look beyond our human differences to unite in Christ.

Establishing cordial, meaningful relationships with each other is made easy because we see each other not through our eyes, but through the eyes of Christ who was willing to lay down His life for His friends.

We show we are one in Christ and we all are His blood-washed and blood-bought saints. Our evangelism is never frustrated, nor is Christ's witness invalidated due to our petty human divisiveness.

We proclaim God loves and seeks reconciliation with a sin-cursed humanity. We can celebrate our diversity by treating each other with the utmost respect, acceptance, and honor. Here, our fellowship is never optional—it is compulsory.

The world craves this unifying message of acceptance of others through Christ, which offers us a glimpse of what Heaven will be like with its rich diversity of people united under the lordship of Jesus Christ. John saw our future in this context, while he was on the Isle of Patmos:

> After this I beheld, and, lo, a great multitude, which no man [or woman] could number, of all nations, and kindreds, and people, and tongues, stood before the throne, and before the Lamb,

clothed with white robes, and palms in their hands; And cried with a loud voice, saying, Salvation to our God which sitteth upon the throne, and unto the Lamb (Revelation 7:9–10 KJV).

Because we are all precious in the sight of the Lord, we can view each other through His loving eyes.

We Love One Another

The word "love" has many meanings today. It names our emotional attraction toward someone or something like our friends, jobs, houses, cars, pop music, pizza, and that old favorite pair of slippers.

The ancient Greeks distinguished parental love (Greek: *storge*)[18] from fraternal love (Greek: *phileo*)[19] from the passion between lovers (Greek: *eros*).[20]

Yet, the Lord established a "new" love when He commanded us to love (Greek: *agape*) each other

---

[18]Walter Bauer, "στέργω," *A Greek-English Lexicon of the New Testament and Other Early Christian Literature*, revised and edited by F. Wilbur Gingrich and Frederick W. Danker, 2nd ed. (Chicago: University of Chicago, 1979) 766.

[19]W.E. Vine, "*phileō*," *An Expository Dictionary of New Testament Words*, in *Vine's Expository Dictionary of Biblical Words*, rev. ed. (Nashville: Thomas Nelson, 1985) 382.

[20]Bauer, "ἔρως,"311.

unselfishly, just as He loves us.[21] His Spirit enables us to express this selfless, pure love consistently, which will confirm we belong to Him (John 13:34–35).

We can express His love as we yield to His Spirit, who instinctively responds to others through us in the ways that serve their best interests. In our strength alone, we are incapable of this altruistic love.

Our human love is inadequate because, with it, we always want to know "What's in it for us?" before we respond. But God demonstrated His unselfish love in Christ toward us, and now He empowers and mandates us to share it with other people.

Here, Christ supplies us with His unquenchable desire to forgive, reconcile, and extend ourselves at all times. This is the "most excellent way" that Paul outlined in 1 Corinthians 13 (**the Love Chapter**).

This unselfish love is patient and kind. It is always at work, seeking opportunities to show kindness on our behalf when we are ready to receive. This love is not jealous, boastful, proud, or rude (v. 4).

Possessiveness or irritability is never present because the giver is never concerned about what

---

[21]See: Bauer, "ἀγάπη," 5, and A.T. Robertson, *A Grammar of the Greek New Testament in the Light of Historical Research*, 4th ed., (Nashville: Broadman, 1934) 65, 115.

the recipient does or does not do "to deserve it." Otherwise, it is no longer love, but it becomes a loan instead.

Love does not demand its own way; it is not irritable and keeps no record of wrongs (v. 5). It is not glad about injustice but is glad when the truth wins out (v. 6). Here, we do not rejoice when wicked triumphs. Our concern is for everyone because we know as one suffers, we all suffer.

Love never gives up, it never loses faith, it is ever hopeful, and it endures (v. 7). Of these three—faith, hope, and love—the greatest of these is love (v 13).

Love is not abstract, but practical, in the sense we do not perform it in secret but extend it in our acceptance, benevolence, and forgiveness toward others.

We Forgive One Another

As equals, we can forgive and forget offenses because God forgave and forgot ours at Calvary. The Lord commands us to express His kindness toward others, especially those who need our forgiveness.

Forgiveness is never easy. But Jesus warns it *is required* to secure God's forgiveness for our offenses. This implies we extend forgiveness equally — to those who ask us for forgiveness — and to those who *do not* ask us for forgiveness.

To forgive means we do not use social media to degrade or humiliate the people we want to "pay back" for hurts we've perceived or experienced. God holds us accountable for our malevolence (whether done maliciously or in jest). Besides, we would not want someone to degrade or humiliate us even if they felt justified to do so.

To forgive also means we do not keep a record of past wrongs as some self-appointed vigilante. If all of us did this, there would be no one left standing since we are equal debtors. The Lord rightly says in John 8:7 (NIV): "Let any one of you who is without sin be the first to throw a stone...."

In addition, to forgive means we do not lash out with verbal or physical attacks against someone who cuts in front of us when we are standing in line, or we are in vehicular traffic. We extend grace to the other person as our equal who happens to be sharing a very brief "flash" of our space and time (compared to the vast eternity we have yet to live).

Lately, I've noticed the increase in social and political attacks against elected officials when the Bible teaches in Romans 13 that we are to pray for and support them (even when they do not share our political views or ideology).

We should apply the principle of extending radical forgiveness, just as we have received and benefitted from it to all other areas of our daily, human interaction.

The Unforgiving Servant failed to do so and suffered the consequences as the Forgiving King imposed punishment and revoked the mercy he had extended. The Bible rightly teaches, "It is a terrible thing to fall into the hands of the living God." (Hebrews 10:31 NLT)

Before we explore Radical Forgiveness in the next chapter, let's continue John and Joanne's story.

> John tried to reach his agent many times to no avail. But when John finally reached him, he scheduled a meeting at his office to confront him about the withdrawals.
>
> During that meeting, John was made aware of the "fine print" of his initial contract, which authorized his agent to serve as his power of attorney.
>
> John also read where all the bonus money earned from his third contract would be paid to the agent as a one-time commission bonus.
>
> "You mean my signing bonus went to you?" John asked. "Yep! You should have read the fine print!" said the agent.

"How do I pay bills, take care of my kids' college, and provide for my family?" John continued.

"That is not my problem, is it?" retorted the agent, and with that, John left the office.

Devastated, John and Joanne prayed about the situation asking God for direction. They shared the news with their family and met with their pastor to pray about finding God's solution.

Their pastor counseled them to forgive the agent, although painful. Then, the Lord could "show himself strong" on their behalf. Reluctantly and painfully, they did.

Chapter Five

Chapter 5
On To Radical Forgiveness

 God forgives us unselfishly and completely, and He expects us to forgive in like manner. It is possible to share His radical forgiveness that transforms others and us as we live out our true freedom in Christ.

Our Freedom in Christ

The word "freedom" conjures ideas of unlimited action without external hindrance or restraint. But in John 8:34–36 (NLT), Jesus teaches freedom has even a far greater meaning:

> I tell you the truth, everyone who sins is a slave of sin. A slave is not a permanent member of the family, but a son is part of the family forever. So if the Son sets you free, you are truly free.

Jesus is teaching that although no one is "cracking a whip" to cause one to sin, continual sin reveals the identity of one's true "master."

Galatians 5:19–21 (NLT) outlines the despicable tasks (or *Lusts of the Flesh*) we perform for our master including sexual immorality, impurity, lustful pleasures, idolatry, sorcery, hostility, quarreling, jealousy, outbursts of anger, selfish ambition, dissension, division, envy, drunkenness, and wild parties.

In addition, pride, which Proverbs 6:17–19 lists among the six characteristics the Lord "hates," serves as another cruel taskmaster whose sole purpose is to forgo forgiveness at all costs. Unrelenting, it forever whispers ever so seductively: *"I've been hurt, so I can't forgive you!"*

Moreover, the residual effects—guilt and shame—hinder us from expressing positive, constructive feelings toward others through acts of hostility, malevolence, selfishness, or unforgiveness as well.

Here it's worth noting that Luke's parallel account of the Parable of the Unforgiving Servant (Luke 17:3) states: "take heed" (Greek: ***prosecho***), which in a broader sense means to "be concerned about, care for, and pay attention to." In this context, it summons our vigilance to: "be [especially] careful," or to "be on guard."[22]

Such introspection helps to free us from pride, selfishness, and the emotional and psychological scars associated with a tragic past as the Lord provides us with the comfort we need (Psalm 30:5 and Revelation 21:4 KJV).

Over time, we affirm there is no condemnation for those who are in Christ. We grow in His grace by walking (not according to the flesh but) according

---

[22] See: Bauer, "προσέχω," 714.

to the Spirit. We also yearn for more of the abundant life He freely extends to all of us who trust in Him for spiritual life and nourishment (Romans 8:1, 2 Peter 3:18, John 10:10).

The Enemy (or *Devil*) uses our spiritual, emotional, and psychological baggage to perpetuate the lie we are worthless and cannot be forgiven.

I've served people who have struggled to forgive themselves and have insisted: "God can't forgive me... *You don't know what I've done!*" We cannot change our past with its hurts. What's been done has been done.

Nevertheless, God created us, and He knows us better than we know ourselves. He is fully aware of our hurts and those "secret" sins no one else knows about. If God is willing to love, accept, treasure, value, and forgive us through Christ, we should be more than willing to love, accept, treasure, value, and forgive ourselves.[23]

Freedom in Christ is the foundation on which our being, identity, choices, and destiny are forever changed.

---

[23] Also participation in a Christian clinical treatment or recovery program in conjunction with a church discipleship or mentoring program can aid in healing from acute physical or emotional abuse or compulsive and addictive behavior by helping us to develop a support and accountability network needed to sustain our healing and wholeness.

We Are Crucified With Christ

"Crucified with Christ" may seem odd or masochistic, but it is not. It is the victorious, Spirit-filled life that allows God's people to live free from the bondage of sin, guilt, shame, and unforgiveness through His blood, as Paul writes:

> I am crucified with Christ: nevertheless I live; yet not I, but Christ liveth in me: and the life which I now live in the flesh I live by the faith of the Son of God, who loved me, and gave Himself for me (Galatians 2:20 KJV).

As members of a local church, we have experienced God's love and forgiveness through Christ so that we can share it with others. In this way, we perform the "ministry of reconciliation" outlined in 2 Corinthians 5:18. God reconciled us to Himself through Christ and empowers us to reconcile with others.

Here, the three-step process outlined in Matthew 18:15–17 can serve as our guide:

1. Contact the offended person(s) for reconciliation.
2. Use a mediator or mediators to help clarify the issue(s) to everyone's understanding.
3. Utilize appropriate local church leadership (i.e., pastors, deacons, elders, etc.), who are

led by the Spirit to resolve the matter through the Word of God and prayer.[24]

Performing the ministry of reconciliation while taking heed to forgive (and forget) our past blunders will help us participate in a lifelong process of spiritual wholeness as illustrated here:

Our Lifelong Process of Spiritual Wholeness

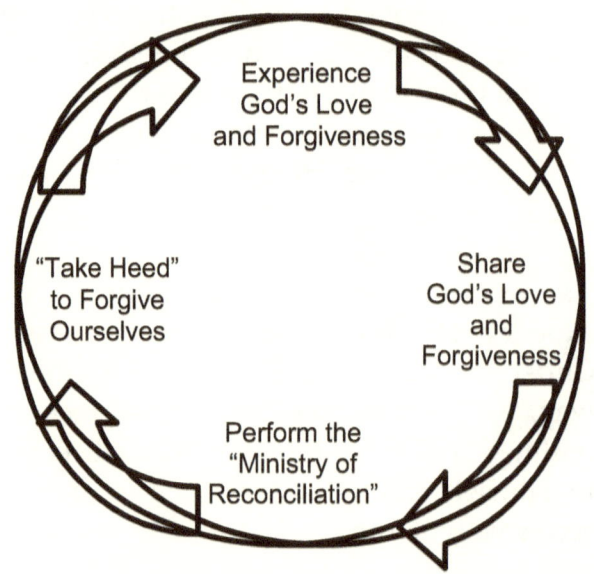

This process will allow us to express more of the *Fruit of the Spirit* as listed in Galatians 5:22–23 (NLT): Love, joy, peace, patience, kindness, goodness, faithfulness, gentleness, and self-control

---

[24]Separation is used only as a last resort. It is better to part ways or "agree to disagree" than to have adversarial factions within close proximity where anger, hostility, strife, gossip, or slander disrupts overall group harmony.

and many other noble characteristics—including forgiveness.

Psalm 139:14 tells us we are "fearfully and wonderfully made" by God, and it would benefit us greatly to see ourselves from His perspective as the unique and significant parts of His wonderful master plan.

We are not mistakes or afterthoughts because God created us to fulfill His perfect, eternal design. Each day features a new opportunity for the Lord to "reset" our lives and circumstances to accommodate His perfect will for us:

> The faithful love of the LORD never ends! His mercies never cease. Great is His faithfulness; His mercies begin afresh each morning. I say to myself, "The LORD is my inheritance; therefore, I will hope in him!" (Lamentations 3:22–24 NLT)

Confident that our forgiving, omnipotent, loving and faithful God will provide His absolute best for us in every situation, we can move on to radical forgiveness.

On To Radical Forgiveness

We show His righteousness, grace, and love through our worship, service, and fellowship. Death is the ultimate price anyone can pay to show love, as we would hardly die for a stranger or a known enemy. Yet, the Lord Jesus Christ did that for us at Calvary, and His Spirit inside us supplies us with the ability to love as He did.

This divine love enables us to extend radical forgiveness to humans everywhere as we:

> - Forgive those who have wronged us without exception or limit
> - Reconcile with those we have wronged

This paradigm shift from the "natural" interpersonal relationship model sounds as revolutionary today as it did two thousand years ago because it not only accepts human imperfections, it also anticipates and embraces them as well. These writers note:

> Ironically, while we cannot change our past we do have the ability to dramatically impact the pasts of others. We do that through forgiveness...Forgiveness necessitates a decision to slice out that part of our history—that event, that action which breached our relationship with the other person involved. We may not forget it but we can decide that it will not preclude our future relationship...Finally, forgiveness involves beginning again...It may not be quick. And the relationship may be rebuilt in a different way than it was before the conflict.

Nevertheless, a rebuilding process begins that can ultimately lead to reconciliation and renewed relationship...We know the biblical instruction on forgiveness. In Matthew, we are instructed to forgive, and told that as we forgive, our Father will forgive us. If we fail to forgive, there is the clear indication that He will not forgive us. That is not an easy passage to accept, but it's one that reflects the necessity of forgiveness in our relationships.[25]

Jesus taught it will be our love that gives substance to our Christian witness and makes it an attractive alternative to a dying world.

We emulate this perfect love by forgiving intentional and unintentional wrongdoings, showing mercy instead of judgment, and extending goodwill toward others in need.

When we express radical forgiveness, we live rightly in the eyes of God and humanity. In God's eyes, we are His children and can experience and express His glory. To humanity, we are the brilliant reflections of God's practical and tangible love, which proves we belong to His Son, Jesus Christ.

---

[25]L. Randolph Lowery, J.D., and Richard W. Meyers, "Capturing the Value of Relationships," *Conflict Management and Counseling*, in *Resources for Christian Counselors* series, vol. 29, no. 6, ed., Gary R. Collins, (Dallas: Word, 1991) 79–80.

We should never think it strange to express radical forgiveness. Our Forgiving King extended it to us, and He transforms us into receptacles of grace and mercy so that we can extend it to others.

In this book, we explored radical forgiveness through the eyes of Jesus. I pray that as we apply these principles, the world becomes a better place for all of us to live in civility.

Before closing the book, let's turn our attention to John and Joanne.

> The next day, John met an attorney to review the contract. They found a clause that released John "after payment of the one-time commission bonus." John contacted his agent to exercise the clause and dissolved the contract. He also told him that all was forgiven.
>
> Years passed, and without their knowledge, John and Joanne's relatives raised college funds for all three children and supplied them with money for their household expenses as well.
>
> John retired as an All-Pro, having set many records over his twenty-year football career. He was nominated to be enshrined into Pro Football's Hall of Fame.

On the way to church one wintery Sunday, John and Joanne saw a homeless man walking in the snow. Moved with compassion, they stopped to take him to their church's homeless shelter. But, when they approached him, they were surprised to learn it was the agent who had become penniless after he was boycotted by other disgruntled clients and "blacklisted" by the league.

John befriended the agent and arranged for his food, shelter, transportation, and employment. Greatly touched by John's compassion, the agent eventually gives his heart to Christ and becomes an active church member.

John, Joanne, and the agent grow into the best of friends over the years; today, they attend the graduation of John and Joanne's youngest child who had studied to become a medical doctor in town.

John was accepted into the Pro Football Hall of Fame. Next month, his former agent—now his best friend—will be his introductory speaker.

About the Author

A product of a Christian home, Floyd Bland has dedicated his life to serving the Lord Jesus Christ primarily as a pastor-teacher and ministry leader.

Through Not Of The World Ministries, Inc., Floyd continues to present sound, practical, Bible-based, interactive learning models for Christian living to help strengthen other Christians in their walk with the Lord and other believers. His other works include *Five Things Every Christian Must Know*, and *The Christian Heritage: Answers for a Searching World*.

Floyd is married to his best friend and helpmate. Together they are blessed to have two grown children and a grandson.

www.ingramcontent.com/pod-product-compliance
Lightning Source LLC
Chambersburg PA
CBHW020430010526
44118CB00010B/504